UNBELIEVABLE!

34 AMAZING FACTS ABOUT ALIENS

Tracy Sue Walker

Lerner Publications ◆ Minneapolis

For Melanie and Doug Knauff

Lerner Publications Company
An imprint of Lerner Publishing Group, Inc.
241 First Avenue North
Minneapolis, MN 55401 USA

For reading levels and more information, look up this title at www.lernerbooks.com.

Main body text set in ITC Franklin Gothic Std.
Typeface provided by Adobe Systems.

Editor: Angel Kidd **Designer:** Mary Ross **Photo Editor:** Angel Kidd
Lerner team: Sue Marquis

Library of Congress Cataloging-in-Publication Data

Names: Walker, Tracy Sue author
Title: 34 amazing facts about aliens / Tracy Sue Walker.
Other titles: Thirty-four amazing facts about aliens
Description: Minneapolis, MN : Lerner Publications, [2026] | Series: Unbelievable! (Updog books) | Includes bibliographical references and index. | Audience: Ages 8–11 | Audience: Grades 2–3 | Summary: "From strange lights in the sky to ancient incredible sites, alien stories have always fascinated humans. Readers discover what a UFO really is, how scientists are looking for aliens, and more in this exciting book"— Provided by publisher.
Identifiers: LCCN 2025013208 (print) | LCCN 2025013209 (ebook) | ISBN 9798765689714 library binding | ISBN 9798348029470 paperback | ISBN 9798765699508 epub
Subjects: LCSH: Extraterrestrial beings—Juvenile literature | Unidentified flying objects—Juvenile literature
Classification: LCC QB54 .W1777 2026 (print) | LCC QB54 (ebook)

LC record available at https://lccn.loc.gov/2025013208
LC ebook record available at https://lccn.loc.gov/2025013209

Manufactured in the United States of America
1-1012510-54839-5/5/2025

Table of Contents

ALIENS ON EARTH?

Scientists haven't found proof that aliens exist. But many believe they do!

The Nazca Lines are giant shapes carved into the ground. They are in Peru.

Some people think aliens created the Nazca Lines.

The pyramids in Egypt are over four thousand years old. Some people believe aliens showed humans how to build them.

Many people think alien bodies are stored in a place called Area 51 in Nevada.

The Extraterrestrial Highway is also in Nevada. It is 98 miles (158 km) long. People have seen a lot of UFOs in this area.

Up Next!

IN THE SKY.

UFOS

UFO means "unidentified flying object."

Some people believe aliens from other planets fly UFOs.

A UFO can be any unknown aircraft.

Many things look like UFOs but are not. Planets, rockets, and drones are some examples.

Between 1948 and 1969, there were more than twelve thousand UFO sightings.

Many differently shaped UFOs have been spotted. Round is the most common shape.

LIST BREAK!

Do you know where people see the most UFOs? Here are the top five states!

1. California
2. Florida
3. Washington
4. Texas
5. New York

Do you know what UFO shapes people see most often? These five shapes are the most common.

1. Round or Sphere: 47 percent
2. Lights or Orbs: 16 percent
3. Oval: 3 percent
4. Cylinder: 2 percent
5. Disc: 2 percent

Up Next!

WHAT'S OUT THERE?

SEARCHING FOR ALIENS

Scientists are searching for aliens.

They listen for radio signals or sounds in space.

A probe on Mars

They also send probes to planets in our solar system.

SETI means "search for extraterrestrial intelligence."

Space telescopes help search for signs of life.

SETI scientists look for things such as pulses of light in space.

Why haven't we found aliens? Our technology might not be able to yet.

Up Next!

WHERE DO ALIENS LIVE?

WHERE ALIENS COULD EXIST

There are a lot of places in the universe where life could exist.

An exoplanet is a planet outside our solar system. Aliens might exist there.

NASA scientists think other planets with life couldn't be too close or too far from the stars they orbit.

Scientists also think a planet with life would need water on it.

An exoplanet

As scientists find more exoplanets, they learn about what life on different planets could look like.

Right now, we can't say for sure that aliens exist.

Glossary

aircraft: any machine that can fly through the air

extraterrestrial: something that exists outside Earth

orbit: the path an object takes around another object

probe: a tool used to explore something that cannot be seen easily

solar system: a group of planets that spins around one star

unidentified: mysterious or unknown

Check It Out!

Betts, Bruce, PhD. *Are We Alone? Searching for Life Beyond Earth with the Planetary Society*. Lerner Publications, 2026.

Britannica Kids: Alien
https://kids.britannica.com/kids/article/alien/399331

Deniston, Natalie. *Aliens*. Jump!, 2025.

ESA Kids: Life Around Other Stars
https://www.esa.int/kids/en/learn/Life_in_Space/Are_we_alone/Life_around_other_stars

NASA Space Place: What Is an Exoplanet?
https://spaceplace.nasa.gov/all-about-exoplanets/en/

Watson, Olivia. *Is There Alien Life in Outer Space? Discover the Science behind Astrobiology*. Beetle Books, 2025.

Index

Photo Acknowledgments

Image credits: Kiyoshi Takahase Segundo/Alamy, pp. 3, 17 (bottom); David Wall/Getty Images, p. 4; Aaron Oberlander/Getty Images, p. 5; Maria Swärd/Getty Images, p. 6; Ratnakorn Piyasirisorost/Getty Images, p. 7; Roger Holden/Getty Images, p. 8; AlizadaStudios/Getty Images, p. 9; Anton Petrus/Getty Images, pp. 10, 12; VICTOR HABBICK VISIONS/ SCIENCE PHOTO LIBRARY/Getty Images, p. 11; Richard Newstead/Getty Images, p. 13; Bettmann/Getty Images, pp. 14–15; FotografiaBasica/ Getty Images, p. 16; David Wall/Getty Images, p. 17 (top) ; Yuga Kurita/ Getty Images, p. 18; NASA/Getty Images, p. 19; NASA/JPL-Caltech, p. 20; jamesbenet/Getty Images, p. 21; NASA/ARC/Eric James, p. 22; NEMES LASZLO/SCIENCE PHOTO LIBRARY/Getty Images, p. 23; NASA/JPL/STScI Hubble Deep Field Team, p. 24; NASA/Ames Research Center/Daniel Rutter, p. 25; NASA/Petigura/UC Berkeley, Howard/UH-Manoa, Marcy/ UC Berkeley, p. 26; RyanTangPhoto/Getty Images, p. 27; NASA's Goddard Space Flight Center, p. 28; Apostoli Rossella/Getty Images, p. 29.

Cover image: KTSDesign/SCIENCEPHOTOLIBRARY/Getty Images.